FACING EAST,
PRAYING WEST

FACING EAST, PRAYING WEST

Poetic Reflections on
The Spiritual Exercises

KENT IRA GROFF

PAULIST PRESS
New York/Mahwah, NJ

Cover design by Sharyn Banks
Book design by Lynn Else

Library of Congress Cataloging-in-Publication Data

Groff, Kent Ira.
    Facing east, praying west : poetic reflections on The spiritual exercises / Kent Ira Groff.
        p. cm.
    Includes bibliographical references.
    ISBN 978-0-8091-4628-4 (alk. paper)
    1. Ignatius, of Loyola, Saint, 1491–1556. Exercitia spiritualia. 2. Christian poetry. 3. Meditations. I. Title.
    BX2179.L8G76 2010
    242′.802—dc22

                                                                    2009042468

Published by Paulist Press
997 Macarthur Boulevard
Mahwah, New Jersey 07430

www.paulistpress.com

Printed and bound in the
United States of America

Table of Contents

TABLE OF CONTENTS

TABLE OF CONTENTS

With gratitude for

Carl L. Dincher, SJ,
Jesu Bhavan, Jamshedpur, India

Edwin J. Sanders, SJ,
Jesuit Spiritual Center, Wernersville, Pennsylvania, United States

Marian Dolores Frantz, IHM
Annunciation Convent, Bellmawr, New Jersey, United States

Orientation

Journey into *The Spiritual Exercises*

Ignatius of Loyola designed the *Spiritual Exercises* for use over four weeks or over periods in a thirty-day retreat (or as a retreat in daily life over several months). The exercises were designed to be used in consultation with a spiritual guide. Whether you have little or lots of knowledge about Ignatius, I offer this brief sketch to clear the path so you can freely follow the Love that leads to life.

Use of imagination is a key feature of the *Exercises*, which emerged from Ignatius's traumatic leg injury in battle at age twenty-six. During his long recovery, he couldn't find any war and love stories of knightly valor to alleviate his boredom. So he began reading lives of saints and gospel stories of Christ. It's as if Ignatius created his own imaginary stage, visualizing scenes and conversing with characters. In contrast to fleeting impressions from chivalrous stories, he experienced lasting effects of consolations from his own imaginative re-creations of gospel scenes.

Each weekly grouping of the *Exercises* involves praying with scriptures using *imagination, intellect, will,* and *emotions,* as we become participants in the Christ-life. We follow the four "movements" or weeks of the biblical story and of our human experience of creation, living, dying, and rising to new life:

Creation: Beautiful Yet Broken. The Word of Love creates the universe and humans, with each of us beautiful and unique, yet alienated and homesick.

Incarnation: Embodying Love. The Word of Love is embodied in the birth, life, and ministry of Jesus' teaching and healing, serving and celebrating.

Crucifixion: Dying to New Life. The Word of Love dies rejected, broken, and forsaken, at one with our own human struggles.

Resurrection: Resilient Love. The Word of Love rises and explodes into new life in us and in the cosmos as we join God's purpose.

In this way the *Exercises* provides an integrative method for many learning modes and varied traditions. It's like a book on how to swim. Some benefit will come from reading it, but far more from practicing in the water.

Poetry encourages such imaginative integration through conversing with self, life, and God—which Ignatius calls *colloquies.* I recount my own journey into Ignatian spirituality as you prepare for this prayerful poetic adaptation.

My Odyssey into the *Exercises*

Most of my theological education focused on learning *about* rather than on *experiencing* God—with no courses in prayer or the spiritual life in my five years at two theological seminaries in the 1960s. After two decades as a pastor, I left parish ministry disheartened. My burnt-out soul was ripe for a way of prayer that would integrate mind and heart, scripture and life, contemplation and action.

During a transitional period as a hospital chaplain, I met a Jesuit priest who became my first spiritual director and introduced me to the *Exercises.* Learning that a person in active occupation could make the retreat over several months, this format fit with my many involvements. I had begun training for ministries in retreat and spiritual direction at Shalem Institute in Bethesda, Maryland. During the same period I founded Oasis

Ministries for Spiritual Development, a nonprofit organization to train others in contemplative active life. Later I participated in eight-day and four-day versions of the *Exercises* to renew my soul. Then I designed and directed one-day introductory sessions by dividing a day into four periods. At this point I had not still participated in the traditional thirty-day retreat.

My retreat exercises began to resonate with my travel experiences and concerns for the world. During a "traveling" peace seminar in the Middle East, I sensed Jesus' continued sufferings amid the destructive and constructive forces of human life. Receiving hospitality with an extended family in a traditional Kenyan village felt like being hosted by Christ. On pilgrimages to the Iona community in Scotland and the Taizé community in France, I sensed connections to the birth, death, and resurrection of civilizations. Walking muddy hills with K'echi' people in Guatemala and eating the women's fresh-baked tortillas seemed like supper in the Upper Room. In such "traveling classrooms" a prayer poem would emerge in my journal to focus my impressions of hope or the impact of despair.

How did this poetic form of the *Exercises* come about? In 1999 I finally got a long awaited sabbatical to make the thirty-day retreat in a country I longed to see—India. I was fortunate to find as my director a Jesuit who, I would learn, had been a close friend of Jesuit author Anthony de Mello, as well as the spiritual director for Mother Teresa during much of her life.

After a time in Calcutta, I arrived at Jesu Bhavan (House of Jesus) in Jamshedpur to begin my retreat during the Hindu feast of Saraswati, goddess of wisdom. I couldn't sleep at night with the loud music, barking dogs, chants from mosques in the wee hours, the roar of planes and trains in the day. I got annoyed. It was anything but contemplative; a retreat meant rest, but I couldn't.

An avalanche of poems began cascading within my head. What to do? *Just be still*, I told myself. Sometimes I would crawl out of bed through my mosquito net in the dark (there was no electricity during the night) and scribble a poem—maybe then I'd be rid of its addictive phrases so I could sleep. Then another poem would occur, like this one:

> At 4 a.m.
> I am not sure
> if the blare I hear
> is the sound of a mosque
> or a fierce mosquito
> near my ear.
> But I am sure
> it is a call to prayer.

I met with my spiritual director and complained about the noise and these poems that kept my mind abuzz when I *should* have been emptying the mind. He told how English Jesuit Gerard Manley Hopkins burned his poetry for pride's sake, but new poems gushed forth, which were published after Hopkins died. My guide reminded me of his late friend Anthony de Mello's phrase to describe the first week of the *Exercises*: "Let the child in you come forth."

We concluded that one of the ways I "play" is to play with words. I mentioned a rabbinic saying that the Sabbath is to play and to pray. Since Ignatius encourages the retreatant to use one's imagination while praying with scriptures, here I was playing *and* praying at the same time! With that, my guide got up and placed his 1950s manual typewriter in my hands, blessing my word-playing as prayer.

Everywhere I prayed I got caught in a web of poems: on dusty streets as children kissed my feet, in a park praying with the text of the wedding at Cana (John 4) and meeting a newly married Hindu couple, on a Muslim's porch by the Subarnarekha

River having tea at sunset. I had written prayer-poems before and have written many since, but India was the fountain.

Why Poetry?
And Ways to Use This Book

Poetry has a way of drawing on intuitive, imaginative, and intellectual dimensions of our response to God's grace, often hidden in undercurrents of desolations and consolations. Letting the flow of words, images, and metaphors out through our fingertips—or in through our eyes—creates a holistic and primal way of praying.

The Book of Psalms is the Bible's prayerbook, and the psalms are poetry. Rabbi Jesus often concluded a story with a Zen-like "take away" line: "The first shall be last and the last shall be first....Leave the dead to bury the dead." Such paradoxical riddles are called "kōans" in Zen tradition. They take you inside yourself. East meets West, intuition greets reason.

In these poems I have not done the work for you; rather, I hope my reflections prepare the fertile soil for the seeds of your own faith, hope, and love to break open—praying and studying alone or with others, on retreat in silence or at a workplace in stress. Their effect may take the form of a spontaneous poem of your own, a surprising act of love, or a serendipitous moment of joy. Think of poetry as a museum that sharpens your eye for some unexpected beauty in the world's grit. You might use this collection:

- For personal prayer and meditation. For example, a poem each morning and evening one day a week for a year.
- With a short-term study, prayer, or support group in

Advent, Lent, or Ordinary Time. For example, as a devotional meditation for committees.
- As a resource for praying the *Exercises* with a spiritual director in any format—eight days, thirty days, or a period of months.
- For two persons sharing a spiritual friendship in person, by e-mail, or by phone.
- As a Bible study focused on renewing baptism and commitment to Christ.

A few particulars may assist your reading. Each prayer-poem is a unique meditation on a scripture or on Ignatius's words. Before each poem I give a related quotation from scripture. After each poem, I give a reference for reflection on the full scripture passage, usually notated as "Scripture reflection." However, this is notated as "Ignatian reflection" in cases where the poem is my meditation on Ignatius's own words in the *Exercises*. Sometimes a scripture also relates to a title in the *Exercises*, notated by an asterisk. If parallel synoptic Gospel texts are cited, usually I list them in order (Matthew, Mark, and/or Luke). As is customary, the *Spiritual Exercises* of St. Ignatius are referred to simply as the *Exercises*.

Baptismal Renewal: Christ in You

To pray the *Exercises* is to renew our baptism into the company of Christ. The essential "exercise" of the spiritual life is living our baptism: that bedrock assurance that God's grace claims us as beloved before we understand it; that Christ walks with us through our living and loving, our wounding and being wounded, our dyings and risings to claim new life and begin again…and again…with purpose.

ORIENTATION

Just as muscles atrophy if not used and we can build up physical strength by adopting a regimen of exercise, the same is true spiritually. By practicing spiritual exercises that internalize Love, we will develop inner resiliency. In this way death opens as a doorway to life, despair becomes an incubator of hope, and reason takes us to the precipice of leaping into "this mystery, which is Christ in you" (Col 1:27).

The Ignatian way seeks to unite action and contemplation with imagination to discern how best to love: Is not that the way of Christ? Is not that the goal of Benedictine, Quaker, or any authentic spiritual path of East or West, North or South? Is it not to practice inner and outer union, that we can say with Gandhi, "My life is my message"? Incarnation means living our baptism. The union of Mary's contemplative hospitality at the feet of Jesus and Martha's active hospitality of service points us to "the one thing necessary," the principle and foundation for living into your unique purpose:

Lord,
keep me doing the One thing
while I do the many things.

Heart of Christ

No one has ever seen God.
It is God the only Son,
who is close to the Father's heart,
who has made him known.
John 1:18

> I will gaze through
> this window into heaven,
> to know as I am known:
> > Eyes of Christ
> > behold me.
> > Hands of Christ
> > enfold me.
> > Face of Christ
> > uplift me.
> > Lips of Christ
> > kiss me.
> > Breath of Christ
> > inspire me.
> > Heart of Christ
> > fire me.
> Body of Christ
> fill me with compassion.
> Lifeblood of Christ
> fill me with your passion
> more now and ever more.

Ignatian reflection: "Soul of Christ," the *Anima Christi*, in the *Exercises* (while meditating on a classic icon of Christ)

Week One
CREATION
Beautiful Yet Broken

In the first "movement," or week, Ignatius emphasizes knowing oneself as a beautiful gift of God's creation, yet also as alienated and broken. Along with Ignatius's numerous scriptural allusions, other texts below are adapted from several versions of the *Exercises* (see bibliography). The choice and order of scriptures highlight the first week's purpose: to focus the heart and mind on being aware—first of the beauty of being deeply loved and then of the fault lines in our experience of love. Ignatius offers two distinctive approaches for our ultimate goal in life and the means of realizing it:

> *Principle and Foundation.* Our goal is to rediscover the purpose for our life: to be loved and to love in return, fully alive to God, self, and others.
>
> *Examen.* Awareness is the heart of the spiritual life and a conscious practice of examining our responses helps us discern how to live and love more wholly.

Principle and Foundation

So God created humankind in his image,
in the image of God he created them;
male and female he created them.
Genesis 1:27

God creates us out of love for love
and desires our eternal wellbeing.
Our response is to embody God's loving
presence and praise by serving fully alive.

All things in this world are given to us
so that we can give back the love we receive.
So we can enjoy these gifts and join God's
purpose by using them to transform the world.
But if we abuse any of creation's gifts or permit
them to control our lives, we need to release
them so that we are wholly free to love.

We can live with equanimity, claiming grace
in abilities or disabilities, failure or success,
praise or criticism, few years or many years.

Let only this desire guide our choices:
What brings God glory by making us
more fully alive to our life's purpose?

Ignatian reflection: "Principle and Foundation," in the *Exercises*

Life Mission Foundation

"If your eye is healthy,* your whole
body will be full of light."
Matthew 6:22

I am
here on this
earth to be a link
between the Word and
the world, a mentor and
message that brokenness
offered to God can be a
source of blessing to
oneself and the
cosmos.

Scripture reflection: Matthew 6:22–33

---

*Single, focused (Greek *haplous*)

An Examen of Grace

Examine yourselves...
1 Corinthians 11:28; 2 Corinthians 13:5

> I invite Christ, Light of the world,
> to walk with me as I scan over
> the past twenty-four hour period
> (or a recent interval), gently sifting
> events, experiences, and encounters.
>
> Gift: I give thanks for some gift(s) of the day.
> I celebrate God's *empowering love* at a time
> or times when I felt loved...or loving...
>
> Struggle: I notice any occasions when
> I struggled to feel loving...or loved...
> an unrest in my soul, something unresolved.
> I celebrate God's *undefeated* love and hear:
> "I know that and I love you. You are my beloved."
>
> Invitation: I ask, what grace is God inviting
> me to name and claim to be more whole...?
> and allow a word or phrase—or an image
> or a metaphor—to come to mind...
> I begin to repeat it slowly, with my breathing...
> or I picture it if it's an image or metaphor...
> I visualize myself in some life situation...
> now acting as if I am already whole.
>
> After meditating, I return to active life
> using a line of a poem, scripture, or song.

(In a group: Share with another person…
End with a brief silent prayer for each other.)

Ignatian reflection: "General Examen of Conscience," in the *Exercises*

Examine Me

O Lord, you have searched me
and known me.
Psalm 139:1

Prayer means getting to know myself
as well as God knows me.

I can only examine my actions
as loving or unloving in relationship
to people—especially when
I get out of my own circle
of familiarity and become
a minority.
            Getting off the bus
at the wrong station in Kisumu,
two eager *metatu** drivers
snatch my precious bags and run
in opposite directions. No phone:
I feel my nothingness in a sea
of Kenyan faces. Is my friend
waiting at another station?
And I—I have nothing
to depend on but eternity.

Scripture reflection: Psalm 139:1–24

---

*Taxi in Swahili

Bare Parable

For I have learned
to be content
with whatever I have.
Philippians 4:11

> To the man in his empty
> room said the bare light
> bulb: I can be as you say.
> Turn me on and I can be bright,
> Turn me off and I can be dark.
> Look at me and I can overwhelm,
> Look at your page and I can illumine.
> Gaze at me one way and I can be stark,
> Gaze at me another and I will show
> you all the hues of the rainbow.

Scripture reflection: Philippians 4:11–13

Spiritual Exercises

But now thus says the Lord,
he who created you, O Jacob, *
he who formed you, O Israel: **
Do not fear, for I have redeemed you;
I have called you by name.
Isaiah 43:1

> The grace that I seek
> in this first week
> is to see myself
> as God sees me.
> This may engender sorrow,
> humility, gratitude, or awe.
>
> I will kneel down and fall
> prostrate this morning,
> stand to sing *!gracias!* at noon:
> And tonight I will fling
> my hands to the heavens
> and say, Ah! and Alleluia!

Scripture reflection: Isaiah 43:1–4; 49:15–16; James 4:6–10

---

*Hear your first name

**Hear your full name

India's Virgin Love

Mary treasured all these words
and pondered them in her heart.
Luke 2:19

> I sit beneath the light-skinned
> Virgin's statue, on her wall,
> in dark-skinned India,
> pondering as she holds her
> Child and fresh dahlia garland
> (the very one that night before
> was draped on me and I wore
> it lavishly when I gave the lecture
> at Morning Star Seminary
> in Barrackpore): How bedrock
> it is to listen to Love
> and allow myself
> to be held—and how simple
> to give love—yet so extremely
> difficult to discern how,
> by what means, and where.
> But who? That is not the problem.

Scripture reflection: Luke 2:19–51

Sitting in Pictures

"Whatever you ask for in prayer,
believe that you have received it,
and it will be yours."
Mark 11:24 (Matthew 21:22)

The Hopi not only dance for rain,
they sit and picture clouds swelling,
streams gushing.
                    When Ignatius invites
us to compose the scene by imagining
the place, the smells, the sights,
the sounds—houses, synagogues,
villages, and crowds with hopes welling
within—it's prayer with visual,
sensual, mental images. It's seeing
the mountain appear to disappear
in the mind's eye: no disembodied
spirituality here.
                    Prayer is sitting
in pictures with scriptures
till they come alive: the hungry
child will thrive, terror of the masses
turn to ashes—then to a mound
of seedlings.

Scripture reflection: Matthew 21:20–22 (Mark 11:20–24)

Yesterday, Today, Tomorrow

How great…are the riches of this mystery,
which is Christ in you, the hope of glory.
Colossians 1:27

> I imagine Christ—lavishly, joyously
> living, forgiving, loving, giving his life.
>
> How have I responded to Christ in my life?
> I picture scenes along my journey to the present:
> scan over events, see hints of following and dallying.
>
> How am I responding to Christ in my life?
> I visualize scenes of recent days and now:
> see myself acting, honoring my desires and God's.
>
> How am I being invited to respond to Christ in my life?
> I imagine scenarios and how they may unwind,
> still focusing on Christ in heart and mind and will.

Scripture reflection: Colossians 1:24–29; 2:6–7

Parable Power

[David] said to Nathan,
"As the Lord lives,
the man who has done
this deserves to die
…because he had no pity."
Nathan said to David,
"You are the man."
2 Samuel 12:6–7

Tell the truth: but do arrange
for it to sneak in from backstage.

When prophet Nathan told King David
of a rich man stealing a poor man's little ewe,
raging anger in the king's heart grew.
But when Nathan said, "That man is you,"
the monarch saw himself and knew
the only thing that he could do
was tell his truth and break his heart
and through his weakness start
anew.
So when you hear another's sin
you can choose: Great power lies within
to see instead a weakness in yourself
as strength, and anger turns
to God and good at length.

Scripture reflection: 2 Samuel 12:1–15

Re-Turning My Gaze

"Two men went up to the temple to pray,
one a Pharisee and the other a tax collector."
Luke 18:10

Sin is not a greater distance;
it is turning your gaze
in the wrong direction
and forgetting who you are.

The Pharisee
turned his gaze
to his own self
and his successes
standing by himself:
"God, I thank you that I am
not like other people…"

When I stand
by myself
I turn my gaze
downward on others
and endanger
my self by myself.

But the tax collector
stood at a distance
(sin is not the greater distance),
but turned his gaze
toward his heart
and God and his sins,
standing as one with all.

When I turn my gaze
toward my heart
it returns to God
and I am no longer
standing alone but
one with the whole
of sweating humanity's
sweltering masses.

I am befriended by the Holy One
that I may be friend to every one.

Scripture reflection: Luke 18:9–14

Hell
Still Alive

"Child, remember that during your
lifetime you received your good things,
and Lazarus in like manner evil things."
Luke 16:25

The theme I hear in
this meditation on Lazarus
in Hades is an experience
of the rich man's unquenchable
fire of remorse: an irreversible
desire to have extended
love and compassion
that can never be retrieved.

Except for me it can:
I am still alive.

Scripture reflection: Luke 16:19–31

Prayer Means

Pray without ceasing.
1 Thessalonians 5:17

> Prayer is going to God by any means
> by any means to let God come to you.
>
> To pray is to yearn:
> tell me your yearnings
> and I'll tell you your prayers.
>
> Pray always,
> pray all ways.

Scripture reflection: 1 Thessalonians 5:16–25

Simon the Tourist

"Simon, I have something to say to you…"
Luke 7:40

> "…about your attitude of superiority,
> your sense of hospitality."
>
> The tourist experienced the most
> lavish welcome in the homes
> of the poor (and when he almost
> lost his valuables, was rescued by his host),
> but complained about the noisiness,
> inefficiency, dirtiness, dust, and mess.
>
> When he returned home
> he pitched the contents
> of his refrigerator

15

in the garbage disposal
and set the grass clippings
from his one acre lawn
out by the street with the trash.
On the way to his first day
at work he turned up
the CD in his car full blast,
and on his cell phone refused
a request to host a refugee family,
saying he had spent all his money.

Scripture reflection: Luke 7:36–50

Me Without You

Why is it, O sea, that you flee?
O Jordan, that you turn back?
O mountains, that you skip like rams?
O hills, like lambs?
Psalm 114:5–6

"Me without you, what would that be like?
You without me, would either of us be?

You would not have peaks and I would not flow,
You would not be high and I would not be low.

I would not draw wild eagles and you would not harbor
    fish;
people would not climb me and boats could not sail on
    you.

You need my softness to flow and to move;
I need your hardness to push and resist.

Said the mountain to the river in the valley,
Without you I would not be a mountain.

Said the river in the valley to the mountain on high,
Without you there would be no river in a valley.

Me without you would not be me,
and you without me would be a different you."

Scripture reflection: Psalm 114:3–8

Found & Lost

"Rejoice with me, for I have
found the sheep that was lost."
"Rejoice with me, for I have
found the coin that I had lost."
Luke 15:6, 9

> Once I am found
> I need to get lost
> again: in Wonder
> Love, and Praise.

Scripture reflection: Luke 15:1–10

Prodigal Mother

"You are always with me,
and all that is mine is yours."
Luke 15:31

"I am your mother's birthpangs
and your own borning cry,
I am unconscious Love
bringing you back to yourself,
I am hope as it rises within
to draw your soul home,
I am the silent wisdom
of the forgiving father,
I am the hidden mother
of every prodigal child:
Will you turn to embrace me
as the father embraced you?
And what of your angry
sister or brother? How
will you embrace the other?"

Scripture reflection: Luke 15:11–32

Kindom* Castle

"Whoever becomes humble like this child
is the greatest in the kingdom of heaven.
Whoever welcomes one such child welcomes me."
Matthew 18:4

> Kindom Castle
> The soul door that leads into
> kindom castle is child-sized:
> generals' brass gets stripped,
> politicians lose all their clout,
> even royalty has to dismount,
> then bishops drop their staffs,
> CEOS have to bow and scrape,
> and intellectuals for the first time
> have their heads lower than their
> hearts and all   of God's kin rub
> arms with the   poor en masse.

Scripture reflection: Matthew 18:4–5 (Mark 9:37; Luke 9:48)

---

*kindom (kingdom): a new human family

Week Two

INCARNATION
Embodying Love

In the second movement of the *Exercises* we discover the stages of our journey mirrored in Jesus' birth, life, temptations, and ministry in our own experiences of joys and struggles. The poetic meditations below generally follow Ignatius's ordering of scriptures for the second week, beginning with the angel Gabriel's announcement to Mary and ending with Jesus' joyful entry into Jerusalem.

We are called to embody a rhythm of contemplating and manifesting the life-changing words and deeds of Jesus. Since the week will crescendo toward Jesus' choice to encounter the forces of life and death, Ignatius provides three classic approaches for discerning difficult choices to live and love more wholly.

> *Two Standards (or Powers).* We are constantly called to make choices for the power of life over death.
> *Three Kinds of Persons (or Selves).* Awareness leads to understanding how we respond to Christ, from procrastinating to compromising to committing.

Discerning Life's Choices. Ignatius examines three occasions for choosing well: when the will is moved to know instantly; when we go through desolations and consolations (up one day, down the next); and in times of tranquility, when we feel no strong pull either way.

Expectant

"For nothing will be impossible
with God."
Luke 1:37

> How can I entertain this
> impossible possibility?
>
> "Be expectant
> without expectations."
>
> "Here am I, the servant of the Lord:
> Let it be with me according to your word."

Scripture reflection: Luke 1:37–38

Mary Colloquy

"Blessed are you and blessed
is the fruit of your womb.
And why has this happened to me,
that the mother of my Lord comes to me?"
Luke 1:42–43

> As a child I remember
> the minister preaching
> how Catholics make so much of you
> while Protestants make so little of you.
> Since I have always been
> on the side of making

much of women
and their too often hidden
work and suffering, and since
my mother's name was Mary,
I have felt your affinity and unity
with all down-trodden
women who gather wood
and carry jugs on heads,
whose bodies are violated
just so that their children
can eat by day and sleep by night.

And I feel your kinship with that hidden
side of me that feels and falls and follows
where this pondering heart shall lead me.
"And a sword shall pierce your own soul too."

"Greetings, favored one!
The Lord is with you."
"Blessed are you among women,
and blessed is the fruit
of your womb"—Jesus.

"My soul magnifies the Lord,
and my spirit rejoices in God my Savior…
He has brought down the powerful
from their thrones and lifted up the lowly."

Help me to cultivate your pondering
heart, your holy art of wondering.

Scripture reflection: Luke 1:26–56; 2:19, 35

Revolutionary Magnificat

[The Mighty One] has brought down
the powerful from their thrones,
and lifted up the lowly.
Luke 1:52

    This Magnificat is revolutionary:

    When a Nazi army
    encircled an Austrian
    village one Holy Saturday
    (but did not consider what day
    the next would be)
    and church bells rang
    Easter hymns at dawn,
    the enemy army (thinking
    many troops had gathered
    overnight) fled with
    Alleluias at their heels.

    Our praise will be the thing
    wherein we'll catch
    the consciousness of the king,
    bring peace instead of warring ways.

Scripture reflection: Luke 1:46–55; 1 Samuel 2:1–10

All Things to All

To the weak I became weak,
so that I might win the weak.
I have become all things

to all people, that I might
by all means save some.
1 Corinthians 9:22

> "Only if you enter their door
> can you exit the door of Christ,"
> said the mentor, referring
> to a Jesuit missionary
> who, centuries ago, wore
> beads and had his ears
> pierced like the people
> he loved while bearing
> reproach from hierarchy above.

Scripture reflection: 1 Corinthians 9:19–23; John 1:1–14

Dream Selves

An angel of the Lord appeared to him
in a dream and said, "Joseph, son of David,
do not be afraid to take Mary as your wife."
Matthew 1:20

> I meditate on Joseph's night
> dreams and my own fright.
>
> I am but a leaky
> bucket of dream fragments,
> each with a bit of half
> remembered and forgotten
> bliss or fear,
> my scattered selves—
> expansive, dismissive, aggressive,

flying around looking
down at me, laughing at me—
myself yelling at them,
begging,

"Don't chop yourself in pieces!
Get inside each one and come home:
get inside the Palestinian orphan,
the imprisoned Israeli soldier,
the shriveled widow with her gold pen,
the wailing Irish grandmother,
the Guatemalan landlord,
the car's wrecked rear fender,
the Taj Mahal's mirror pools,
the kids and kin on Baghdad's streets,
the African boy with AIDS—
the whole bulldozed refugee camp."

Marry each one to the marrow
of your bone and come home.

Awake.

Scripture reflection: Matthew 1:18—2:23

Glory to God in the Lowest

"Glory to God in the highest
heaven, and on earth peace…"
Luke 2:14

> "What good is it for the Christ
> to be born two thousand years ago
> if Christ is not born in you?"

Meister Eckhart would ask
of us in century twenty-one.

If I cannot enter into real fears:
rumors of a child's illegitimacy,
dislocation of unfair taxation,
estrangement of a manger,
how can I celebrate the angel's
announcement,
"Fear not!"?

How can I sing, "Glory to God in the highest!"
unless I share the pain of the lowest?

Only by working for justice and peace on earth
can I dare rejoice at this Savior's birth.

Scripture reflection: Luke 2:1–14

Facing East, Praying West

Wise men* from the East
came to Jerusalem, asking,
"Where is the child who
has been born king of the Jews?"
Matthew 2:1–2

Magi from the East magnify
the feast of Incarnation:
Word made flesh where

---

*Magi in Greek

East meets West: intuition
greets reason, silence
enfleshes presence, contemplation
embodies manifestation:

"The silent Word is pleading,"
facing east, praying west:
　　　　Epiphany!

This treasured Christ
is bathed with Light
from the ancient East.

Scripture reflection: Matthew 2:1–12

Refugee Status

An angel of the Lord appeared
to Joseph in a dream and said,
"Get up, take the child
and his mother, and flee to Egypt."
Matthew 2:13

　　"Egypt" does not
　　close its borders
　　when the holy family
　　declares refugee status.

　　Once back in "Nazareth"
　　home folks still insist
　　on permanent alien cards.

Scripture reflection: Matthew 2:13–23; Mark 6:1–6

Jesus in the Temple

When [Jesus] was twelve
years old, they went up
as usual for the festival.
When the festival was ended…
the boy Jesus stayed behind.
Luke 2:42–43

> Jesus at twelve in the temple
> answered with wisdom simple:
> "Did you not know that I must
> be about my Father's interests?"

> This youth had wandered;
> now his mother pondered.

> What are the passages
> of *your* life
> and what are their messages?

Scripture reflection: Luke 2:41–51

Spartan Preparation

The voice of one crying
out in the wilderness:
"Prepare the way of the Lord."
Matthew 3:3

> I am blest by the Baptist's austerity:
> wearing leather girdle, sandals,
> eating locusts, honey in the wild.
> Simplicity prepares the roaming child

in me to greet the humble Christ
in this third world community.

O drench me
in this Sun by day
and I shall revel
in your candle
Light by night.

Scripture reflection: Matthew 3:1–12 (Mark 1:2–8; Luke 3:1–20;
John 1:6–14)

"You Are My Beloved"

And a voice came from heaven,
"You are my Son, my beloved;
with you I am well pleased."
Mark 1:11

But how can I ever feel beloved?
That was Christ, your unique son.
And I am certainly not the one
in whom you are well pleased.

Since you are baptized into Christ,
hear this same word with a twist:
"You are my beloved daughter
or son—with unique genes
and DNA and life experiences!

To know I am well pleased in you,
now turn to me each moment new."

Scripture reflection: Matthew 3:13–17 (Mark 1:9–11; Luke 3:21–22)

Baptized into Wilderness

And the Spirit immediately drove
him out into the wilderness....
and he was with wild beasts;
and the angels waited on him.
Mark 1:12, 13b

Baptize my heart in your wild love! Though restless
still, as your beloved child I will enter into wilderness.

Sure I will struggle with these beasts
and long to see you in the least:
for there I taste the angel's feast.

Scripture reflection: Mark 1:12–13

Night Demons

No testing has overtaken you
that is not common to everyone.
1 Corinthians 10:13

They come in the night,
these demons of self-doubt
—they come to disqualify me,
kidnapping my confidence:
How can you be spiritual
yet be this anxious?
How dare you offer
your needy self to be
a spiritual guide for others?

Then the Spirit comes
to fortify me with
the ancient assurance:
that I am one beggar
showing other beggars
where to find bread,
that my very neediness
validates my credentials,
as one who surely seeks
and just as surely finds
—as one already found.

Scripture reflection: 1 Corinthians 10:11–13; Mark 1:12–13

Jubilee Beyond

"The Spirit of the Lord is upon me,
because he has anointed me
to bring good news to the poor."
Luke 4:18

In Nazareth Christ
proclaims the year of Jubilee:
Give sight to blind,
let lame ones walk,
preach good news
to the have-not folk
and set the captives free.

And it was Christ in me,
driven to cliff-hanger fears,
who whispered in the jeers,
"No good thing here

can you do; only few respond.
Your freedom lies beyond,
a broader place, another year."

God grace me
in what grief I find
to grow in love
in heart and mind
till I embody Jubilee.

Scripture reflection: Luke 4:16–30

Come and See

Rabbi: "What are you looking for?"
Disciples: "Where are you staying?"
Rabbi: "Come and see."
John 1:38–39

When Jesus says,
"Come, follow me,"
it's always
"Come and see."

Never obligation,
only invitation
to transformation:
lifelong vocation.

Scripture reflection: John 1:35–51 (Matthew 4:18–22; Mark 1:16–20;
Luke 5:1–11)

Two Kinds of Power I*
Free for Love

"No one can serve two masters, for a slave
will either hate the one and love the other,
or be devoted to the one and despise the other.
You cannot serve God and wealth."
Matthew 6:24 (Luke 16:13)

> Align me with all people
> and purposes that promote
> the reign of Christ.
>
> Disarm me from all
> that works against
> Christ's cause.
>
> Then I shall gain a heart
> set free for love and praise.

Scripture reflection: Matthew 6:19–24 (Luke 16:10–13)

Two Kinds of Power II**
Choose Life!

I have set before you life and death,
blessings and curses. Choose life
so that you and your descendants may live,

---

*Meditating on Ignatius's "Two Standards"

**Meditating again on Ignatius's "Two Standards"

35

loving and serving the Lord your God.
Deuteronomy 30:19–20

> God! How—tell me!—can some choose life
> when death has chosen them through
> AIDS, earthquakes, tornadoes?
> Do others *choose* the curse of addictions,
> when statistically some are more at risk
> by being poor, homeless, lost on city streets?

> Ah, but I can choose to choose life on their behalf,
> and power to live and give as one on loan to all:
> for Christ no longer calls us slaves but friends.

> God! I vow not to choose death and power that enslaves,
> but to choose the Christ life that empowers and saves.

Scripture reflection: Deuteronomy 30:16–20

Three Kinds of Selves*

Another said, "I will follow you, Lord;
but let me first say farewell to those at my home."
Jesus said to him, "No one who puts a hand to the plow
and looks back is fit for the kingdom of heaven."
Luke 9:61–62

> Admirers hug the shore, applauding those who swim,
> and yet it's always, "Nah, another day" for them.

> Waders try the water but never quite get in,
> yet for fear of what, it's never really clear.

---

*Meditating on Ignatius's "Three Classes of Persons"

Swimmers give themselves to water's flow
and in the giving are supported as they pull
—and release. Ah, here is faith Mysterious:

You never really hold it,
yet you're held by it.

I observe these selves in me:
How does admirer change to follower?
It seems I start by wading into a cause
—then fear of what others
think evaporates as I hear
Christ calling out within me:
"I need *you* now and here."

O Love Supreme,
transform me
from sometime
through maybe
to now.

Scripture reflection: Luke 9:57–62 (Matthew 8:19–22)

Into the Deep

*"Put out into the deep water
and let down the nets."*
Luke 5:4

When something keeps emerging
on the shore line of the mind
be sure to notice, not submerge it.

"Put out into the deep
and let go of the nets,"
the Guru's voice instructs.

"But I have tried to let go
here for days and nights."

"Ah, here you are so close
to shore the thing is magnified.
And when you cast in shallows
your self gets caught and tied."

When I embrace my fears,
move out into the deep,
the object that consumed me,
incredibly disappears.

Let go—these nets
that tangled you for years
are free to drop and draw
new life and energy.

Scripture reflection: Luke 5:1–11

Wedding Light

Jesus said to them,
"Fill the jars with water."
And they filled them up to the brim.
John 2:7

At this glorious wedding
feast of West and East,
shedding Light on Love's best
gifts received and given,

stands shadowed
Mary facing West:
"Your joy is gone,"
she says while always
pointing toward her Son:
"Whatever he tells you
do it." Messiah Jesu
now commands:
"Fill the jars…

Fill the jars with stories
    that sparkle with surprise,
    the ferment of suspense…
Fill the jars with music,
    the rhythms of grace
    in drum and dance…
Fill the jars with ordinary
    drops of experience,
    holy silence…
    joy in sacrifice."

This steward
may yet announce,
"You have saved
the best till last."

Scripture reflection: John 2:1–11

Outrageous Love

"Zeal for your house
will consume me."
John 2:17

> What causes me outrage
> and how do I engage
> the powers that abuse
> simple beauty of the world,
> defiling this temple
> globe and all God's people,
> stealing its ozone and its food?

Scripture reflection: John 2:13–22 (Matthew 21:10–17;
Mark 15–19; Luke 19:45–48)

Plain Preaching

And he came down with them
and stood on a level place...*
And he looked up at his disciples and said:
"Blessed are you who are poor...
Blessed are you who are hungry...
Blessed are you who weep now...
Woe to you who are rich...
Woe to you who are full now...
Woe to you who are laughing now..."
Luke 6:17, 20–21, 24–25

---

*level place or plain (King James Version)

When I recount these
blessings and their woes
they seem irrational
and impossible:

How can poor be rich,
the hungry full,
and mourners laugh?

What crazy grace rewards its foes
and damns possessions or success?

I possess within what I allow to pass
along; non-possessing leads to blessing.

Jesu, I will stand beside you
on this level plain to share
in all whose pain you bear.

Scripture reflection: Luke 6:20–36

Be Attitude Aware

"Blessed are the poor in spirit,
for theirs is the kingdom of heaven."
Matthew 5:3

For good reason Jesus' "blesseds"
are called "beatitudes" and their
opposite is treason. For hate
betrays an attitude unaware.

Let this be my attitude
in making peace my aim,

in taking risks for works
of justice and compassion:
to get inside the skin
of all God's kin to listen
to their pain and passion
and thereby know my own.

If all be lost yet I shall gain
this kindom* joy of heaven
    now and then.

Scripture reflection: Matthew 5:1–12

---

*kindom (kingdom): a new human family

The Vase

Mary… sat at the Lord's feet…
Luke 10:39

> I pray for
> the grace
> to sit at
> the feet
> of each
> person I meet
> and see Christ
> in their face.

Scripture reflection: Luke 10:38–42

Luke's Good News

"Therefore I tell you, do not worry
about your life, what you will eat,
or about your body, what you shall wear."
Luke 12:22

Try this for Christology:

Lord Jesus as you show
us to live life from below:
cradle manger,
pulpit boat,
temple mountain,
eating bread at others' tables,
befriending Prodigal and Samaritan,
not a place to lay your head,
gambled robe,
Roman cross,
borrowed tomb,
still rising from the dead,
revealing friend in stranger,
known in breaking bread,
giving life forgiving love:

Now I raise doxology:

Let me treasure how I borrow
life today to love tomorrow.

Scripture reflection: The Gospel of Luke, chapters 1 through 24

Love and Pain

"Therefore, I tell you, her sins,
which were many, have been
forgiven. Hence she has shown
great love.
Luke 7:47

My young Chinese artist
host plays music on his car radio.
I like it and ask, "What are the words?"
He pauses—
"Love and pain."

How is it life's one cosmic soup
of love and pain?
Someone with pain of rejection
loves forgiveness's restoration.
Jesus parties
with folks with little—yet wastes
it all for love—and ends
with not a thing.

Love and pain—
then love—
life's song. Again...

Scripture reflection: Luke 7:36–50

Claiming Crumbs

And his disciples came and urged him, saying,
"Send her away, for she keeps shouting after us."
He answered, "I was sent only
to the lost sheep of the house of Israel..."
She said, "Yes, Lord, yet even the dogs
eat the crumbs that fall from the master's table."
Matthew 15:23–24, 27

This fearless Canaanite shouter
will not take No for an answer,
pleading for her troubled daughter.

That Bread may bear another's name,
but she will surely claim her crumb.

Yet how much silence she endured
before she boldly stormed the Lord.

Scripture reflection: Matthew 15:21–28 (Mark 7:24–30)

Baptizing Stress

"I have a baptism with which to be baptized,
and what stress I am under until it is completed!"
Luke 12:50

I was baptized under stress
with this Jesus whose crucifix
I now fondle in the fingers
of my mind's eye as I caress
this certain hope: Resurrexit!

Scripture reflection: Luke 12:49–50

What Keeps Bothering Me

"Because this widow keeps bothering me,
I will grant her justice, so that she may
not wear me out by continually coming."
Luke 18:5

> The miracle
> is that what keeps
> bothering me keeps
> me continually coming.

Scripture reflection: Luke 18:1–8

There & Here

Then Peter said to Jesus, "Lord,
it is good for us to be here."
Matthew 17:4

> You can't get there from here.
> Only if you stay
> with each here and discover
> a way
> to embrace its fear
> can you listen for
> the seed of hope within the horror
> or the terror.
>
> You can't get here from there.
> By dwelling
> on a future place, an outgrown year,

you fail to be aware
in this space, this here,
and you will miss
the seed of joy within the anger
or the languor.

You will find that living
into the present—
the question this day,
the struggle this moment,
you will inch your way
along into some amazing answer—
then serendipitously, miraculously,
you will discover
that you are there.

But you will not see
it along the way,
and even in arriving
at your destiny
you will not find yourself saying,
"Now I am there,"
but only
what you have been practicing
each day:

It is good to be here.

Scripture reflection: Matthew 17:1–8 (Mark 9:2–8; Luke 9:28–36)

Rich Young Controller

A certain ruler asked him,
"Good Teacher, what must I do
to inherit eternal life?"
Luke 18:18 (Matthew 19:16)

"Good Guru,
what deed must I do
to gain immortality?"
asked the young CEO
who never lacked
for anything including
a smart question.

"Why call me good
when only God
is good? Do no harm
to anyone and live
the laws of Love,"
answered Guru Jesu.

"All these I am able
to manage quite well."

"One thing you lack
is lacking one thing.

Give up control
to ones who have not.
Live with your want
and in the emptiness

_____

49

you will gain eternal
Presence."

The young controller went away sad,
afraid of losing all he thought he had.

O Guru Jesu: Teach me your ways
that I may follow you all my days.

Scripture reflection: Matthew 19:16–23 (Mark 10:17–22; Luke 18:18–23)

The Voice

"My sheep hear my voice.
I know them, and they follow me."
John 10:27

It is so difficult to listen
to the Voice instead
of the voices—the ones
that rattle around
in my own head,
and the marketeers
announcing, Buy this!
You need that! Come here,
go there! Sell your self.

How can I listen for that still
small voice to find
my own voice?

Ah, Be still and know…
God is *still*…
speaking.
God is still
speaking…

Scripture reflection: John 10:1–10

Rehearse the Exercises

with the story of Lazarus's
dying and being raised.

       One.
"The Father and I are one,"
we read in John chapter ten,
verse thirty, the core of week one:
Each of us is born in union
with God—and yet alienation
seeps in and we're incurably homesick.

       Two.
"I have shown you many good
works from the Father. For which
of these are you going to stone me?"
reads chapter ten, verse thirty two.
Week two silhouettes Jesus' ministry,
escalating with gathering intensity:
acts of love trigger political hates.
News from his home away from home:
Lazarus, brother of Martha and Mary,

is dead. (Mary's the one who anointed
his feet: real ministry means receiving
love, not just healing, teaching, giving.)

    Three.
"Let us also go, that we may die with him,"
says Thomas in chapter eleven, verse sixteen.
"Lazarus is dead. For your sake I am glad…":
What Zen-like nonsense does this Jesus speak?
Yet it's the essence of tragedy this third week.

    Four.
Jesus said to her, "I am the resurrection and the life."
The mystery's complete in eleven, verse eight.
"Come out!" Jesus' voice is a choice for Lazarus
and for all who would follow these exercises
of dying to what is fake and rising to take
and receive—and remember to give back.

Scripture reflection: John 10:30—11:44

Courageous Extravagance

Since there will never cease to be some
in need on the earth, I therefore command you,
"Open your hand to the poor and needy neighbor."
Deuteronomy 15:11

In the house of Simon the leper, these words are engraved forever
on the Table of the Lord's Supper:
IN REMEMBRANCE OF HER
She opened her extravagant hand,
poor woman to poor Son of Man,
who opened the extravagant hand
of God to the poor of every land.

Scripture reflection: Matthew 26:6–13; Deuteronomy 15:7–11

Triumphal Distractions

A very large crowd spread their cloaks
on the road, and others cut branches
from trees and spread them on the road.
And the crowds that went ahead of him
and that followed were shouting…
"Blessed is the one who comes
in the name of the Lord!
Hosanna in the highest heaven!"
Matthew 21:8–9

> I try to pray that I can pray
> with blaring noises, horns and sirens,
> shrills of rickshaws, trucks and scooters,
> booming music, planes and trains,
> children's voices playing, crying,
> trills of birds in palms and mangoes.
>
> Hosanna in the highest!
> shout these voices of the lowest.
>
> What are these braying sounds I hear
> from the stable below my chapel loft?
> I close my eyes and visualize the scene:
>
> Christ now mounts
> the foal that pants beneath me,
>   its ooMooMooMooM…
>   becomes the Om…
>   of all creation.
> I enter holy city's center,
> Rabbi Jesus cleanses temple.

Hollywood cannot create this set:
you only close your eyes and let
such dogged sounds be holy hounds
of heaven in a temple of contemplation.

Scripture reflection: Matthew 21:1–11 (Mark 11:1–11;
Luke 19:28–40; John 12:12–19)

Choosing Well,
Living Whole

Be transformed by the renewing of your minds,
so that you may discern what is the will of God—
what is good and acceptable and perfect.
Romans 12:2

Sometimes choosing is like
a ship going straight to port:
no hesitation or negotiation:
the heart's Desire is clear.

Sometimes choosing is like
sailing with an untoward wind—
the pulls of consolations,
the counter-pulls of desolations.
But, Ah! You tack into the stress;
with skill you follow your bliss.

Other times there's no movement.
You're dead in the water: you yearn
for disturbance or assurance yet
get only deafening echoes of apathy.

Then is when you take the challenge
to chart an inner course to change:
gather information—facts and feelings;
picture the choice in your mind's eye,
then weigh its pros and cons.

Imagine a colleague in your shoes,
what do you say to help the person choose?
Imagine yourself at the end of life:
what choice gives inward peace, less strife?
With Gandhi, picture the poorest person
in the world—then make your decision.

Present your Self wholly to God:
How does this choice sit
with your head, your heart,
and the pattern of your faith journey?

Ignatian reflection: "Three Occasions for a Wise and Good Choice"
in the *Exercises*

Week Three
CRUCIFIXION
Dying to New Life

Scriptures for the third movement of the *Exercises* begin with Jesus' celebration of the Passover supper with his disciples, followed by praying in the garden, and end with his arrest and violent death at the hands of political, religious, and military leaders under the direction of the Romans—and his burial in a borrowed tomb.

Ignatius's exercises for the birth, life, and ministry of Jesus take up at least twice as many pages as those for the crucifixion. It's also true of the number of chapters in the gospel portraits of Jesus and of the number of poems here. The point is clear: The message of Jesus is not about death but about dying to whatever is false to live wholly and joyfully. The cross is about "poetic justice"—if we live congruent with our true Self, then we will know that justice for the "least of these" brings joy to our own hearts.

The upside-down message of the cross says the Third World is first and the first is third. Embracing Christ in my least likely neighbor means embracing the least parts of one's Self. Like poetry, life rhymes! The *Exercises* focus the imagination on the cross.

Visualizing Christ on the Cross. Though also placed in week one, I offer one form of this life-giving exercise for Week Three, and another for Week Four. Paul says, "I have been crucified with Christ, and it is no longer I who live, but it is Christ who lives in me" (Galatians 2:19–29).

Feetward

"So if I, your Lord and Teacher,
have washed your feet, you also
ought to wash one another's feet."
John 13:14

> Love
> stands
> on
> its
> head:
> Guru*
> washes
> disciples'
> feet.

Scripture reflection: John 13:1–17

*"Teacher" in Sanskrit

Tasting Transformation

Jesus took a loaf of bread, and after
blessing it, he broke it and gave it
to the disciples, and said,
"Take, eat; this is my body."
Then he took the cup, and after giving
thanks he gave it to them, saying,
"Drink from it, all of you."
Matthew 26:26

Christ in Eucharist
takes brokenness
and transforms
our hurts
to
bliss
so we
may bless.

Scripture reflection: Matthew 26:17–30; 1 Corinthians 11:23–26

Real Joy

"You will have pain,
but your pain will turn into joy."
John 16:20

> If you would
> know Joy,
> know Love
> that seeks through pain
> and tracks the rainbow in the rain.

Scripture reflection: John 16:20–22

Gethsemane I
Mere Desire

"Sit here while I pray."
Mark 14:32

> Christ comes to me
> in my lethargy to say,
> "*You* sit here
> while *I* pray."

> When you cannot pray,
> Christ in you will pray.

> Weary soul, know this well: merely
> your desire to pray is already prayer.

Scripture reflection: Matthew 26:36–46 (Mark 14:32–42;
Luke 22:39–46)

Gethsemane II
Sweltering Masses

His sweat became like great drops
of blood falling down on the ground.
Luke 22:44

> I heard a medical explanation
> for your bloody drops of sweat.
> But I get more satisfaction
> and it surely fuels my passion
> that you identify with bloody masses
> and sweltering violence of injustice.

Scripture reflection: Luke 22:39–46 (Matthew 26:36–46;
Mark 14:32–42)

Gethsemane III
Need Desire

"Abba, Father, for you all things
are possible; remove this cup from me;
yet, not what I want, but what you want."
Mark 14:36

> Abba,
> Lead me where I need to go,
> not always where I want to go.
> Ah! But may the path of need
> become the path of my desire:
> the way, the truth, the life,

where gratitude is debt of love
and I am home while on the road.

Scripture reflection: Matthew 26:36–46 (Mark 14:32–42;
Luke 22:39–46)

Jesus Before Pilate

But he gave [Pilate] no answer,
not even to a single charge,
so the governor was greatly amazed.
Matthew 27:14

> Silent statement,
> political action.
>
> Paucity of words,
> audacity in deed.

Scripture reflection: Matthew 27:11–14

Bound to Suffer

"The Son of Man must undergo great
suffering, and be rejected...and be killed,
and after three days rise again."
Mark 8:31

> This Messiah* is just
> bound to suffer
> violence and injustice:

---

*Messiah (Hebrew) and *Christ* (Greek) mean "Anointed One."

Judas's betrayal,
Peter's denial,
Pilate's trial.

"I have been crucified with Christ;*
and it is no longer I who live,
but Christ who lives in me."

This Messiah is just
bound to suffer and rise
out of violence and injustice:
    ethnic mockery,
    religious bigotry,
    political trickery.

"If they kill me, I will live on
in the hopes of my Salvadoran people,"
prophesied Archbishop Oscar Romero.
Amen: and it was so, and so it is.

Scripture reflection: Mark 8:31; 9:31; 10:33; 15:6–47;
Galatians 2:20

Visualizing Jesus on the Cross

"They will look on the one whom they have pierced."
John 19:37

Ponder some brokenness in your own life,
past or present, or some brokenness
in another's life that causes you pain.

---

*Messiah (Hebrew) and *Christ* (Greek) mean "Anointed One."

Now visualize Christ on the cross,
sharing that brokenness with you.
For example, if you are experiencing
physical, emotional pain—or relational pain
with a child, partner, friend, or co-worker—
picture Jesus on the cross sharing the hurt
you feel in relation with yourself or another.
Imagine Jesus with arms outstretched saying:

> "Father, forgive them, for they
> do not know what they are doing."

Crazy Horse's buried heart at Wounded Knee
is part of Christ's pain and mine at injustice
done to Ogala Sioux and all displaced peoples.*
Allow your mind to go to such places of injustice.

Later: picture Christ risen yet still wounded,
saying to you as he said to "doubting" Thomas,

> "Put your finger here and see my hands.
> Reach out your hand and put it in my side."

Imagine wounds in your life being used to transmit
faith and hope and love with persons whom you meet.

Scripture reflection: Luke 23:34; John 20:27

---

*Crazy Horse was a Native American murdered by U.S. military forces in 1877 in South Dakota. His father and mother carried their thirty-five-year-old son's heart and bones to Wounded Knee Creek, honoring his request to "bury my heart at Wounded Knee."

Friday's Saturday

Joseph of Arimathea, who was a disciple of Jesus,
though a secret one because of his fear,…asked Pilate
to let him take away the body of Jesus.
John 19:38

Holy Saturday embraces wholly:
remembered celebrations then
now emptiness and nothingness,
laid to rest on time's hewn rock.

After triumphal marches
into the center of things,
the passionate temple cleansing;
after paradoxical betrayal
and eleventh-hour denial
by inner circle friends;
after religious political
systems eliminate the least of these;
after death deals its caustic blow,
sucks out the hero's passion
till nothing is left but exhaustion—
the warped and mindless body
is placed in borrowed tomb, wrapped
in a shroud, dead to the world.

The running's run,
the risking's done:
the rest begun,
the silence won.

Inhabit this darkling tomb until another day:
a quake will seek a happy fault and will awake
Compassion's daughters to anoint this clay.

Scripture reflection: John 19:38–42 (Matthew 27:57–61;
Mark 15:42–47; Luke 23:50–56)

Week Four
RESURRECTION
Resilient Love

Scriptures for the fourth movement in the *Exercises* begin with Mary Magdalene's and the other women's visit to the empty tomb in the garden and Jesus' surprise appearances to disciples—ending with his disappearance and the coming of the Spirit on the Jewish feast of Pentecost. Resurrection means becoming resilient with love. We begin on this earth to live and love, and give and forgive, and leave our impressions of love to enter life eternal.

One sacred exercise gathers up the intention of the entire journey into Christ, the well-known prayer "Take and Receive" or "Contemplation on Divine Love." On the one hand Ignatius means that we return our gifts to God: "Take, Lord, and receive all…that I have and possess."* On the other hand, the prayer assumes we first "take and receive" God's gift of life in Christ so that we can give everything back to God for the sake of the world. The resurrection-life embodies all this world's blessings so that we may bless the world.

---

*Ignatius's "Contemplation on Divine Love" in the *Exercises*

Contemplation on Divine Love. Ignatius's words express the
   meaning of "the principle and foundation" as I offer
   myself. I have learned to care but not to care: to
   embody Christ's passion and compassion without
   concern for what others think of me as long as I live
   out my unique purpose on earth.

Take to Give, Receive to Love

Take, Lord, and receive
all my liberty, memory, mind,
and will: my wanting, having, doing:
being. For only your life in us
is real—and all this world's
gifts are merely held in trust
for us to use and thus return
your love and give and live.
All things I offer to your service.
Grant me only your love and grace;
for all my days that will suffice.
Gratia! Merci! ¡Gracias!

Ignatian reflection: "Contemplation on Divine Love" in Ignatius's *Exercises*

Magdalene I
Incarnation

Supposing him to be the gardener,
[Mary Magdalene] said to him, "Sir,
if you have carried him away,
tell me where you have laid him…"
Jesus said to her, "Mary!"
John 20:15–16

I ponder.

What if Mary
hadn't spoken
to the gardener?

I wonder.

Scripture reflection: John 20:11–18

Magdalene II
Apostle

Jesus said to her,
"Do not hold on to me."
John 20:17

> "Do not attach to me
> in this experience
> or you will miss
> the next expression
> of my Presence.
>
> But go and tell and show:
> keep the faith by giving it away."

Scripture reflection: John 20:11–18

Marking Baptism

A young man was following him,
wearing nothing but a linen cloth.
They caught hold of him, but he left
the linen cloth and ran off naked....
As they entered the tomb,
they saw a young man,
dressed in a white robe,
sitting on the right side.
Mark 14:51–52; 16:5

I.
Youth is stripped of attachments,
naked during crucifixion.

Youth is clothed in compassion,
announcing resurrection:

"Jesu Guru goes before you
into every hurting place
in every continent and race."

II.
Your baptism closes gaps:
rich poor, global tribal,
East West, male female.

How blessed are you
if as a child you learn
this truth—midlife
and all your days—so that
your youth is renewed
like the eagle's.

O mark me with this sign:
I will resign the old—put on
the new and follow you
into this world community
to pray to work and pray
for peace with justice and equality.

Scripture reflection: Mark 14:51–52; 16:5–7; Colossians 3:9–10

Healing Wounds

Jesus came and stood among them
and said, "Peace be with you."
Then he said to Thomas,
"Put your finger here and see my hands.
Reach out your hand and put it in my side."
John 20:26

I tried for years
to heal with scars,
but love's wounds run
deep. Then One appeared
who knows such pain
as will remain
forever open
yet life giving,
all forgiving.

"Peace be with you,"
came Love's refrain.

I will gladly
keep these wounds
if you will only use

my vulnerable Self as strength
for giving others
faith and hope and love at length.

Scripture reflection: John 20:24–29

Pleased to Feed

Peter felt hurt because he said to him
the third time, "Do you love me?"
And he said to him, "Lord, you know
everything; you know that I love you."
Jesus said to him, "Feed my sheep."
John 21:17

"I am the Bread but you deny
and look for joy another way."

"How many ways do I deny?"

"By apathy,
distractions,
or outright lie."

"Does it feed you that I love you
even though you turn away?"

"Yes, Lord, it feeds me
even as it grieves me."

"Do you love me?
Do you love me?
Do you love me?"

Find your pleasure in this treasure:
"Feed my sheep as you are fed;
lead my flock as you are led;
give back my love:
you shall not lack."

Jesus, Lover Friend:
I will trust in you to hallow
this upside-down Way I follow.

Scripture reflection: John 13:38; 21:15–19

Altar Wings

You have stripped off the old self
with its practices and have
clothed yourselves with the new self.
Colossians 3:9–10

My coiled soul, my foiled self

now springs to

Life:

it is enough

for living resurrection faith.

But if I doubt this mystery,

wherever I see

Love

altaring violence

there is the risen Presence.

Scripture reflection: Colossians 3:1–11

Rickshaw Hut

"Truly I tell you, just as you
did it to one of the least of these
who are members of my family,
you did it to me."
Matthew 25:40

To enter Daniel's roadside
hut I had to bow
removing shoes to walk
on his dirt floor, then lift
my eyes to see the bandaged
rickshaw driver's wounded
head. In thatchéd
shadows there (at
his request) the prayer I said
was feebler than
his weakened frame
from cycle rickshaw accident.

When eyes were opened there,
with glowing teeth and hungering
eyes, stood circled children
with wife at husband's
gentle side—and next to me
my school child friend who
will ride with Daniel once again
when health returns and head
and shoulders heal. Mean
while this school child
is the teacher and the pupil
through whose eyes

my clumsy feet were
privileged to stand
on holy ground
and my hands to pass
some love and bread
within the circle
of his squatter's shed.

O sacred head now wounded,
T'is I deserve your place;
Permit my soul instead
Transmit your love and grace.

Scripture reflection: Matthew 25:31–46

Great Co-Mission

They worshiped him; but some doubted.
And Jesus came and said to them…
"Go therefore and make disciples
of all nations, baptizing them
in the name of the Father and of the Son
and of the Holy Spirit, and teaching them
to obey everything that I have commanded."
Matthew 28:17, 19–20

What crazy leadership strategy
is this?—a little outing back in Galilee,
the place where you began—
now with only twelve minus one
and some still doubting.
I will try and begin again
to hear your great co-mission:

FACING EAST, PRAYING WEST

"Go forth to East and South
and West and North,
no longer slaves but friends:
Follow where I send
to ends of earth to bring to birth
the Love that lures new followers
to mend this universe
where violence rends
afflicted masses from their lands
igniting hate in races and religion
while humans spoil my creation.

You will always know my Presence
if you attend to my command:
Listen to Love to love each other.
Go forth to drench my thirsty
children, severed from their roots,
with a severe Mercy that prunes
the vines to bear Love's fruits:
for the merit of Father, Son, and Spirit:
One God, Mother of us all."

I shall hallow the Creator,
then follow the Christ,
and allow the Counselor
to lead—and serve and love
to bless and so be blest.

Scripture reflection: Matthew 28:16–20

God in All Things

Great Spirit, Grant
us eyes to see thee
God in all things
all things in God:
CONCEALED IN A MANGER
CRUCIFIED ON THE WOOD
REVEALED AS A STRANGER
in Bethlehem's stable
on Golgotha's tree
at Emmaus's table
would we see thee!
Our host and guest
born among beasts
Our most and best
with us as the least:
help us go on doing good
protect each from all danger
and transform us as you would.

Scripture reflection: Luke 24:13–35

Western Reflection

No church shared with me in the matter
of giving and receiving, except you alone.
Philippians 4:15

> I will not try to speak as Indian,
> African, Latin American or Asian.
> Instead I will reflect as Western
> and Christian, which is what I am:
>
> We dream we might have given you
> values without the downside: lasting
> qualities of democracy, liberation,
> equality, technology, and education,
> salvation from the caste-bound class—
> without spoiling the environments.
>
> Instead we gave you plastic bags
> and throw-away consumerism,
> crazy stress and cigarettes,
> a yen for white instead of dark,
> addictive wealth for very few,
> capitalist trends that threaten health.
>
> If only we had never tried to give alone
> but mutually receive and live as one—
> a love to share, a hope to dare,
> a truth to find while being found.
>
> How can it be that I should gain
> an interest in my neighbor's pain—

yet in the same encounter learn
the secret path for which I yearn?

Scripture reflection: Philippians 4:15–20

Can We Be Rooted Yet Open?

All who believed were together
and had all things in common.
Acts 2:44

Sadly, being deeply spiritual often results
in communalism: "We're right, you're wrong,"
and triumphalism: legislating God by fiat.

Yet throwing out the spiritual quest
produces an elite naïveté that fails to see
the deep religious bent of humanity.

India with its "secular" political experiment
is still a veritable hotbed of religious fervor:
even those who say they don't believe, believe.

Or look at the former Soviet government:
repressing religion solidified a deeper drive:
frozen spirits thawed, dividing exponentially.

The U.S. is no different: professing secularism
or agnosticism, scratch an American and you
often find three or four faith colors underneath.

Fundamentalism in any of its streams, religious
or political, is like a bridge without flexibility,
concealing frozen fissures, collapsing in the crossing.

Can there be a genuine spirituality that is rooted
yet opens up the soul instead of closing out?
It is the contemplative active life I must promote.

But where can we find prototype affinities
for twenty-first century faith communities?

Scripture reflection: Acts 2:42–46

Postmodern Retreat

Jesus came and said to them…
"Go therefore and make disciples"…
but some doubted.
Matthew 28:19, 17

>   Here I am:
>   introspective,
>   such yearning grace
>   a learning space
>   needing
>   this place
>   for returning—
>
>   retrospective,
>   noticing
>   remembering
>   integrating
>   rhythms of foiled grace
>   in the risings
>   and the fallings—

contraspective,
    a symphony of
    unbalanced balance
    dissonant notes
    with rests from the score
    of my many selves
    and other lives—

perspective,
    peeking into
    the paradoxical
    terrific terrifying
    comic cosmic
    Mystery—

prospective,
    mining my universe's
    black holes: wedding
    primal knowing
    modern knowledge:
    personal political
    doubting believing
    complex joy
    in simple trust.

Scripture reflection: Matthew 28:16–20; Mark 16:14–15

Turn to God in All Things
A Chant

Kent Ira Groff, 1991 (Spanish translation 2009)
adapted from Ignatius of Loyola and Mechtild of Magdeburg

Kent Ira Groff, 1991
arr. David M. Glasgow, 2009

Bibliography

Bergan, Jacqueline Syrup, and Marie Schwan. *Praying with Ignatius of Loyola*. Winona, Minnesota: St. Mary's Press, 1991.

Dister, John E., SJ. editor. *A New Introduction to the Spiritual Exercises of St. Ignatius*. Collegeville, Minnesota: A Michael Glazier Book, The Liturgical Press, 1993.

Dunne, Tad. *Spiritual Exercises for Today: A Contemporary Presentation of the Classic Spiritual Exercises of Ignatius of Loyola*. San Francisco: HarperSanFrancisco, 1991.

Fleming, David L., SJ. *Draw Me into Your Friendship: The Spiritual Exercises: A Literal Translation and a Contemporary Reading*. St. Louis: The Institute of Jesuit Sources, 1996.

Ganns, George E., SJ. *The Spiritual Exercises of Saint Ignatius: A Translation with Commentary*. St. Louis: The Institute of Jesuit Sources, 1992.

Harter, Michael, SJ. editor. *Hearts on Fire: Praying with the Jesuits*. St. Louis: The Institute of Jesuit Sources, 1993.

Link, Mark, SJ. *Challenge. Journey. Decision* (three volumes): *A Meditation Program Based on the Spiritual Exercises of St. Ignatius*. Valencia, California: Tabor Publications, 1988.

Mattola, Anthony, PhD. translator. *The Spiritual Exercises of St. Ignatius*. New York: Doubleday Image Books, 1964.

Muldoon, Tim. *The Ignatian Workout: Daily Spiritual Exercises for a Healthy Faith*. Chicago: Loyola Press, 2004.